THE USBORNE INTERNET-LINKED

FIRST THOUSAND WORDS

IN JAPANESE

With Internet-linked pronunciation guide

Heather Amery

Illustrated by Stephen Cartwright

Edited by Nicole Irving
and designed by Andy Griffin

Japanese language consultant: Joyce Jenkins, Tomoko Taguchi-Boyd
and Kayoko Yokoyama

About *kana* signs

The words in this book are written in simple Japanese signs, called *kana*. Each *kana* represents a syllable. (A syllable is part of a word that is a separate sound, for example, "today" has two syllables: "to" and "day".)

Below you can see all the *kana* signs and find out which sounds they represent. There are also lots of tips to help you make these sounds like a Japanese person.

Japanese has two sets of *kana* signs, called *hiragana* and *katakana*. *Hiragana* signs are used for the traditional sounds of Japanese. *Katakana* signs are used for words that Japanese has borrowed from other languages, such as "taoru", borrowed from the English word "towel".

Next to each *kana*, you can see a guide to how it is said. In the book, each Japanese word is shown in the same way, that is, in *kana* with a pronunciation guide based on the guides on this page. Japanese also use more complicated signs, called *kanji* or "characters". You can find out about *kanji* on page 56.

Hiragana

あ	a	い	i	う	u	え	e	お	o
か	ka	き	ki	く	ku	け	ke	こ	ko
が	ga	ぎ	gi	ぐ	gu	げ	ge	ご	go
さ	sa	し	shi	す	su	せ	se	そ	so
ざ	za	じ	ji	ず	zu	ぜ	ze	ぞ	zo
た	ta	ち	chi	つ	tsu	て	te	と	to
だ	da			づ	zu	で	de	ど	do
な	na	に	ni	ぬ	nu	ね	ne	の	no
は	ha	ひ	hi	ふ	fu	へ	he	ほ	ho
ば	ba	び	bi	ぶ	bu	べ	be	ぼ	bo
ぱ	pa	ぴ	pi	ぷ	pu	ぺ	pe	ぽ	po
ま	ma	み	mi	む	mu	め	me	も	mo
や	ya			ゆ	yu			よ	yo
ら	ra	り	ri	る	ru	れ	re	ろ	ro
わ	wa							を	(w)o
ん	n								

In the lists above, signs with guides written in slanted letters (*like this*) are based on the ones above.

Katakana

ア	a	イ	i	ウ	u	エ	e	オ	o
カ	ka	キ	ki	ク	ku	ケ	ke	コ	ko
ガ	ga	ギ	gi	グ	gu	ゲ	ge	ゴ	go
サ	sa	シ	shi	ス	su	セ	se	ソ	so
ザ	za	ジ	ji	ズ	zu	ゼ	ze	ゾ	zo
タ	ta	チ	chi	ツ	tsu	テ	te	ト	to
ダ	da			ヅ	zu	デ	de	ド	do
ナ	na	ニ	ni	ヌ	nu	ネ	ne	ノ	no
ハ	ha	ヒ	hi	フ	fu	へ	he	ホ	ho
バ	ba	ビ	bi	ブ	bu	べ	be	ボ	bo
パ	pa	ピ	pi	プ	pu	ペ	pe	ポ	po
マ	ma	ミ	mi	ム	mu	メ	me	モ	mo
ヤ	ya			ユ	yu			ヨ	yo
ラ	ra	リ	ri	ル	ru	レ	re	ロ	ro
ワ	wa							ヲ	(w)o
ン	n								

As you can see, to make this new set of sounds you add a little mark to the *kana*.

Pronunciation tips

Here are a few tips that will help you to say the *kana* signs above in a really Japanese way:

- wherever the pronunciation guide shows **a**, say this like the "a" in "father"
- say **i** like the "ee" in "meet"
- say **u** like the "oo" in "cuckoo"
- say **e** like the "e" in "end"
- say **o** like the "o" in "corn"
- when you see a line over a letter (for example ō), this shows the sound is long.

For other letters, say them as if they were part of an English word, but remember these tips:
- when you see **r**, say it as a soft "r" sound, halfway between an "l" and an "r"
- when you see **g**, say it as in "garden"
- the **(w)o** sound is shown with the "w" in brackets because you sometimes say "wo", and sometimes just "o". In this book, the pronunciation guide for each word will make clear which sound to make
- the **fu** sound is halfway between "foo" and "hoo"
- the **n** sound on its own (at the bottom of each list) a nasal "n" sound, much as if you had a cold.

In English, many words have a part that you stress or say louder. For example, in the word "daisy", you stress "dai". In Japanese, you say each part of the word with the same stress.

On every double page with pictures, there is a little yellow duck to look for. Can you find it?

About this book

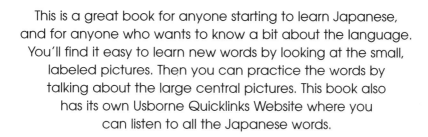

This is a great book for anyone starting to learn Japanese, and for anyone who wants to know a bit about the language. You'll find it easy to learn new words by looking at the small, labeled pictures. Then you can practice the words by talking about the large central pictures. This book also has its own Usborne Quicklinks Website where you can listen to all the Japanese words.

Looking at Japanese words

You will see that Japanese words are written with special signs. You can find out about these on the page opposite and on page 56. It will take you a little time to learn Japanese signs so, to help you, the Japanese word is also written in our alphabet.

Writing in Japanese

Traditionally, Japanese is written from right to left and top to bottom. This means you start a book at what to an American person is the back. In this book, everything is written from left to right, just as in American books.

Saying and listening to Japanese words

Throughout this book you will find an easy how-to-say guide for each Japanese word, but the best way to learn how to speak Japanese is to listen to a Japanese speaker and repeat what you hear. You can listen to all the words in this book, spoken by a Japanese person, on the Usborne Quicklinks Website. Just go to **www.usborne-quicklinks.com** and type in the keywords "1000 japanese". To hear the words, you will need your Web browser (e.g. Internet Explorer or Netscape Navigator) and a program that lets you play sound (such as RealPlayer® or Windows® Media Player). These programs are free and, if you don't already have one of them, you can download them from Usborne Quicklinks. Your computer also needs a sound card but most computers already have one of these. Please read the **Internet note** for parents and guardians on page 56.

A computer is not essential

If you don't have access to the Internet, don't worry. This book is a complete and excellent Japanese word book on its own.

うち uchi

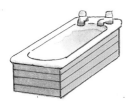

おふろ ofuro

せっけん sekken

じゃぐち jaguchi

トイレット・ペーパー
toiretto-pēpā

ハブラシ ha-burashi

みず mizu

トイレ toire

スポンジ suponji

せんめんだい
senmendai

シャワー shawā

タオル taoru

ベッド beddo

よくしつ yokushitsu

いま ima

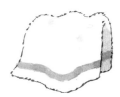

ねりはみがき
neri-hamigaki

ラジオ rajio

クッション
kusshon

シーディー
shiidii

じゅうたん
jūtan

ソファー

4

かけぶとん kakebuton　　くし kushi　　シーツ shiitsu　　しきもの shikimono

ようふくだんす
yōfuku-dansu

まくら makura

ひきだし hikidashi

かがみ kagami

ブラシ burashi

でんきスタンド
denki-sutando

しんしつ
...hitsu

え e

げんかん
...kan

コートかけ kōto-kake

でんわ denwa

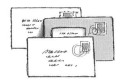

...ター　　ビデオ bideo　　しんぶん shinbun　　テーブル tēburu　　てがみ tegami　　かいだん kaidan

5

れいぞうこ reizōko

コップ koppu

とけい tokei

こしかけ koshikake

こさじ kosaji

スイッチ suicchi

せんざい senzai

かぎ kagi

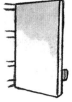

ドア doa

そうじき sōjiki

だいどころ daidokoro

ながし nagas

なべ nabe

フォーク fōku

エプロン epuron

アイロンだい airon-dai

ごみ g

6

ナイフ naifu

モップ moppu

せんたくき hataki

タイル tairu

ほうき hōki

せんたくき sentakuki

ちりとり chiritori

ひきだし hikidashi

うけざら ukezara

フライパン furaipan

レンジ renji

スプーン supūn

おさら osara

アイロン airon

ものいれ mono-ire

ふきん fukin

コーヒーカップ kōhii-kappu

マッチ macchi

ブラシ burashi

ボール bōru

7

にわ niwa

じょうろ

ねこぐるま
neko-guruma

すばこ
su-bako

やかん
katatsumuri

れんが renga

はと hato

スコップ sukkopu

てんとうむし tentō-mushi

ごみいれ gomi-ire

たね tane

こや koya

みみず mimizu

はな hana

ごみいれ
supurinkurā

かなぐわ kana-guwa

すずめば
suzume-ba

すばち subachi

シャベル shaberu

ほね hone

いけがき ike-gaki

またぐわ mataguwa

しばかりき shibakariki

こみち ko-michi

は ha

き ki

けむり kemuri

けむし kemushi

くまで kumade

とりのす tori no su

こえだ ko-eda

くさ kusa

うばぐるま ubaguruma

はしご hashigo

たきび takibi

ホース hōsu

おんしつ onshitsu

まんりき manriki

かみやすり kami-yasuri

ドリル doriru

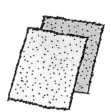

はしご hashigo

のこぎり nakogiri

おがくず ogakuzu

カレンダー karendā

さぎょうば sagyōba

ねじ neji

どうぐばこ dōgu-bako

ねじまわし nejimawashi

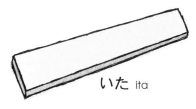

いた ita

かんなくず kanna-kuzu

おりたたみナイフ oritatami-naifu

びょう byō

くも kumo

ボルト boruto

ナット natto

くものす kumo no su

たる taru

はえ hae

おの ono

まきじゃく makijaku

ハンマー hanmā

やすり yasuri

ペンキかん penki-kan

ざいもく zaimoku

くぎ kugi

さぎょうだい sagyōdai

びん bin

かんな kan-na

とおり tōri

バス b

みせ mise

あな ana

きっさてん kissaten

きゅうきゅうしゃ
kyūkyūsha

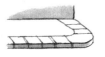

ほどう hodō

アンテナ antena

えんとつ entotsu

やね yane

シャベルカー
shaberu-kā

ホテル hoteru

おとこのひと
otoko-no-hito

パトカー patokā

どかん
dokan

ドリル doriru

がっこう
gakkō

うんどうじ
undō-jō

12

こうつうしんごう
kōtsū-shingō

シー
shii

おうだんほどう
ōdan-hodō

こうじょう
kōjō

トラック torakku

えいがかん eiga-kan

ライトバン raito-ban

ローラー rōrā

トレーラー torērā

いえ ie

いちば ichiba

ふみだん fumidan

オートバイ ōtobai

んしゃ
nsha

しょうぼうしゃ
shōbō-sha

けいかん keikan

くるま kuruma

おんなのひと
onna-no-ko

がいとう
gaitō

アパート apāto

13

おもちゃや
omochaya

ハーモニカ hāmoni

きしゃセット
kisha-setto

さいころ
saikoro

たてぶえ tate-bue

ロボット robotto

ドラム doramu

ネックレス nekkuresu

カメラ kamera

ビーズ biizu

にんぎょう ningyō

ギター gitā

ゆびわ yubiwa

にんぎょうのいえ
ningyō no ie

ふえ
fue

つみき tsumiki

おしろ o-shiro

せんすいかん
sensuikan

トランペット
toranpetto

ゆみ
yumi

ハーモニカ
parashūto

ヨット yotto

かおようえのぐ
kaoyō-enogu

ローラー rōrā

おめん
omen

レーシングカー
rēshingu-kā

もくば mokuba

ちょきんばこ
chokin-bako

ビーだま bii-dama

あやつりにんぎょう
ayatsuri-ningyō

ピアノ piano

うちゅうひこうし
uchū-hikōshi

クレーン kurēn

ねんど nendo

てっぽう
teppō

へいたい heitai

えのぐ enogu

ロケット roketto

15

ぶらんこ buranko

すなば sunaba

ピクニック pikunikku

たこ tako

アイスクリーム
aisukuriimu

いぬ inu

もん mon

こみち ko-michi

かえる kaeru

こうえん kōen

ベンチ benchi

すべりだい
suberidai

おたまじゃくし
otamajakushi

いけ ike

ローラースケート rōrā-sukēto

しげみ shig

かちゃん akachan

スケートボード sukētobōdo

つち tsuchi

うばぐるま ubaguruma

シーソー shiisō

こども kodomo

さんりんしゃ sanrinsha

とり tori

さく saku

ボール bōru

ヨット yotto

いと ito

みずたまり mizu-tamari

こがも ko-gamo

なわとび nawatobi

き ki

かだん kadan

はくちょう hakuchō

ひきづな hikizuna

かも kamo

どうぶつえん dōbutsuen

つばさ tsubasa

わし washi

かば kaba

パンダ panda

ゴリラ gorira

まえあし mae-ashi

カンガルー kanga

こうもり kōmori

さる saru

ひょうざん hyōzan

ペンギン pengin

しっぽ shippo

おおかみ ōkami

わに wani

くま kumo

はね hane

ペリカン perikan

だちょう dachō

イルカ iruka

ライオン raion

らいおんのこ raion-no-ko

キリン kirin

つの tsuno

らくだ rakuda

あざらし azarashi

しか shika

しろくま shiro-kuma

かめ kame

ぞうのはな zō no hana

さい sai

ぞう zō

バッファロー baffarō

ビーバー biibā

しまうま shima-uma

へび hebi

やぎ yagi

さめ same

くじら kujira

とら tora

ひょう hyō

19

せんろ senro

きかんしゃ hikan-sha

くるまどめ
kuruma-dome

しゃりよう sharyō

うんてんしゅ untenshu

かしゃ kasha

プラットホーム
puratto-hōmu

しゃしょう shashō

スーツケース
sūtsukēsu

きっぷはんばいき
kippu-hanbaiki

りょこう ryokō

ヘリコプター herikoputā

えき eki

ガソリンスタンド gasorin-sutando

しんごう
shingō

リュックサック
ryukkusakku

ヘッドライト
heddo-raito

エンジン enjin

しゃりん sharin

バッテ
batt

20

ひこうき　hikōki

スチュワーデス　suchuwādesu

かっそうろ　kassōro

かんせいとう　kanseitō

こうじょう　hikōjō

スチュワード　suchuwādo

パイロット　pairotto

せんしゃ　sensha

トランク　toranku

ガソリン　gasorin

レッカーしゃ　rekkā-sha

せんしゃ

ガソリンしゃ　gasorin-sha

スパナ　supana

タイヤ　taiya

ボンネット　bon-neto

オイル　oiru

ガソリンいれ　gasorin-ire

ふうしゃごや
fūsha-goya

ねつききゅう
netsu-kikyū

ちょうちょ
chō-cho

とかげ tokage

いし ishi

きつね kitsune

おがわ ogawa

みちしるべ
michi-shirube

ちょうちょ
hari-nezumi

いなか inaka

やま yama

すいもん sui-mon

りす risu

もり mori

あなぐま anaguma

かわ kawa

みち mi

テント tento

うんが unga

まるた maruta

むら mura

が ga

はし hashi

ふね fune

たき taki

ふくろう fukurō

トンネル ton-neru

こぎつね kogitsune

もぐら mogura

つりびと tsuri-bito

いわ iwa

ひきがえる hikigaeru

でんしゃ densha

キャンピングカー kyanpingu-kā

おか oka

23

ほしくさのやま
hoshikusa no yama

ぼくようけん
bokuyō-ken

あひる ahiru

こひつじ ko-hitsuji

いけ ike

ひよこ hiyoko

やねうら yane-ura

ぶたごや buta-goya

おうし o-ushi

あひるのこ ahiru no ko

にわとりごや
niwatori-goya

トラクター torakutā

のうじょう nōjō

おんどり ondori

がちょう gachō

タンクローリー tanku-rōrii

なや naya

ぬかるみ
nukarumi

ておしぐる
te-oshi-guru

 うふ nōfu
 そうげん sōgen
 めんどり mendori
こうし ko-ushi
 へい hei
サドル sadoru
 うしごや ushi-goya

 めうし me-ushi

 すき suki

 かじゅえん kaju-en

 うまごや uma-goya

 こぶた ko-buta

 ひつじかい hitsujikai

 しちめんちょう shichimenchō

 かかし kakashi

 のうか nōka

 ほしくさ hoshi-kusa
 ひつじ hitsuji
 わらたば wara-taba
 うま uma
 ぶた buta

25

ヨット yotto

うみ umi

オール ōru

とうだい tōdai

シャベル shaberu

バケツ baketsu

ひとで hitode

すなのしろ
suna no shiro

ビーチパラソル
biichi-parasoru

はた hata

せんいん
sen-in

うみべ umibe

かい kai

かに kani

かもめ kamome

しま shima

モーターボート
mōtā-bōtō

すいじょうスキー
suijō-sukii

なみ nami

ぼうし bōshi

がけ gake

ふね fune

カヌー kanū

ロープ rōpu

こいし koishi

かいそう kaisō

あみ ami

かい kai

つりぶね tsuri-bune

みずかき mizu-kaki

ろば roba

さかな sakana

みずぎ mizugi

オイルタンカー oiru-tankā

はまべ hamabe

ボート bōto

デッキチェアー dekki-cheā

27

はさみ hasami

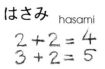

けいさん keisan

けしごむ keshigomu

ものさし monosashi

しゃしん shashin

フェルトペン feruto-pen

がびょう gabyō

えのぐ enogu

おとこのこ otoko no ko

えんぴつ enpitsu

がっこう gakkō

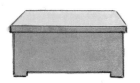

つくえ tsukue

ほん hon

ペン pen

のり nori

チョーク chōku

え e

みばこ
omibako

せんせい sensei

はこ hako

ちず chizu

ふで fude

てんじょう tenjō

かべ kabe

ゆか yuka

ノート nōto

a b c d e f g
h i j k l m n
o p q r s t u
v w x y z

アルファベット
arufabetto

バッジ bajji

すいそう suisō

かみ kami

ブラインド buraindo

a b c d e f g
h i j k l m n
o p q r s t u
v w x y z

のとって
no totte

しょくぶつ
shokubutsu

ちきゅうぎ
chikyūgi

おんなのこ
onna no ko

クレヨン
kureyon

でんきスタンド
denki-sutando

イーゼル iizeru

かんごふ kangofu

だっしめん
dasshimen

くすり kusuri

エレベーター erebētā

ガウン gaun

まつばづえ
matsuba-zue

じょうざい jōzai

おぼん o-bon

うでとけい
ude-dokei

たいおんけい
taionkei

カーテン kāten

びょういん byōin

テディベア
tedibea

りん
ring

ギブス
gibusu

ほうたい hōtai

くるまいす
kuruma-isu

ジグゾーパズル
jiguzō-pazuru

いしゃ isha

ちゅうし
chūs

いしゃ isha

しつないばき shitsunai-baki

コンピューター konpyūtā

バンドエイド bando-eido

バナナ banana

ぶどう budō

かご kago

おもちゃ omocha

なし nashi

カード kādo

おむつ omutsu

つえ tsue

ビ terebi

ねまき nemaki

パジャマ pajama

オレンジ orenji

ティッシュ・ペーパー tisshu-pēpā

まんが manga

まちあいしつ machiai-shitsu

31

ふうせん fūsen

チョコレート chokorēto

おかし okashi

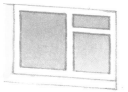

まど mado

はなび hanabi

リボン ribon

ケーキ kēki

パーティー pātii

ストロー sutorō

ろうそく rōsoku

かみぐさり kami-gusari

おもちゃ omo[cha]

みかん mikan

サラミ sarami

カセットテープ
kasetto-tēpu

ソーセージ sōsēji

ポテトチップス
poteto-chippusu

きぐるみ ki-gurumi

さくらんぼ sakuranbo

フルーツジュース
furūtsu-jūsu

きいちご ki-ichigo

いちご ichigo

でんきゅう denkyū

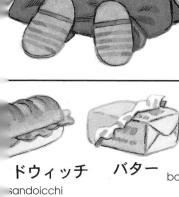
ドウィッチ
sandoicchi

バター batā

ビスケット
bisuketto

チーズ chiizu

パン pan

テーブルクロス
tēburu-kurosu

33

グレープフルーツ
gurēpu-furūtsu

にんじん　ninjin

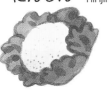

カリフラワー
karifurawā

ねぎ　negi

マッシュルーム
masshurūmu

きゅうり　kyūri

レモン　remon

セロリ　serori

アプリコット
apurikotto

メロン
meron

おみせ omise

かいものぶく
kaimono-buku

チーズ

くだもの と やさい

たまねぎ
tamanegi

キャベツ
kyabetsu

もも　momo

レタス　retasu

さやえんどう
saya-endō

ト
to

34

ご
ago

プラム puramu

こむぎこ
komugiko

はかり hakari

びん bin

にく niku

パイナップル
painappuru

ヨーグルト yōguruto

バスケット basuketto

ボトル botoru

ハンドバッグ
hando-baggu

さいふ saifu

おかね o-kane

かんづめ kanzume

がいも
ga-imo

ほうれんそう
hōrensō

いんげん ingen

レジ reji

かぼちゃ kabocha

カート
kāto

35

たべもの tabemono

あさごはん asa-gohan

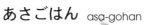

ひるごはん hiru-gohan

ゆでたまご yude-tamago

コーヒー kōhii

めだまやき medama-yaki

トースト tōsuto

ジャム jamu

クリーム kuriimu

ぎゅうにゅう gyūnyū

コーンフレーク kōn-furē ku

ココア koko

さとう satō

はちみつ hachimitsu

しお shio

こしょう kos

こうちゃ kōcha

ティーポット tiipotto

ホットケーキ hotto-kē ki

ロールパン rōru-pan

ばんごはん ban-gohan

ハム hamu

スープ sūpu

オムレツ omuretsu

はし hashi

サラダ sarada

ハンバーガー hanbāgā

とりにく tori-niku

ごはん gohan

ソース sōsu

スパゲッティー supagettii

マッシュポテト masshu-poteto

ピザ piza

フライドポテト furaido-poteto

デザート dezāto

37

わたし watashi

あたま atama

かみ kami

かお kao

うで ude

ひじ hiji

おなか onaka

つまさき tsumasaki

あし ashi

あし ashi

ひざ hiza

まゆげ mayuge

め me

はな hana

ほほ hoho

くち kuchi

くちびる kuchibiru

は ha

した shita

あご ago

みみ mimi

くび kubi

かた kata

むね mune

せなか senaka

おしり oshiri

て te

おやゆび oya-yubi

ゆび yubi

わたしのようふく watashi no yōfuku

クス sokkusu パンツ pantsu ランニングシャツ ranning-shatsu ズボン zubon ジーパン jiipan ティーシャツ tiishatsu

ート sukāto シャツ shatsu ネクタイ nekutai はんズボン hanzubon タイツ taitsu ドレス doresu

セーター sētā トレーナー torēnā カーディガン kādigan マフラー mafurā ハンカチ hankachi

ーカー suniikā くつ kutsu サンダル sandaru ブーツ būtsu てぶくろ tebukuro

ベルト beruto バックル bakkuru ジッパー jippā くつひも kutsuhimo ボタン botan ボタンのあな botan no ana

ケット poketto コート kōto ジャケット jaketto やきゅうぼう yakyū-bō ぼうし bōshi

ひと hito

だんゆう danyū   じょゆう joyū

コック kokku

ダンサー dansā

かしゅ kashu

うちゅうひこうし uchū-hikōshi

けいかん keikan   ふじんけいかん fujin-keikan

にくや nikuya

だいく daiku

しょうぼ
shōbōs

がか gaka

さいばんかん saibankan

せいびし seibishi

びようし biyōshi

トラックのうんてんしゅ
torakku no untenshu

バスのうんてんしゅ
basu no untenshu

エイター
ueitā

ウェイトレス
ueitoresu

ゆうびんや
yūbin-ya

はいしゃ haisha

せんすいふ sensuifu

ペンキや penkiya

パンや panya

かぞく kazoku

むすこ
musuko

おとうと
otōto

むすめ
musume

あね
ane

はは haha
つま tsuma

ちち chichi
おっと otto

おば oba

おじ oji

いとこ itoko

そふ sofu

そぼ sobo

41

どうさ dōsa

ほほえむ hohoemu

なく naku

かんがえる kangaeru

きく kiku

わらう warau

うけとる uket

なげる nageru

こわす kowasu

かく kaku

かく kaku

たたききる tataki-kiru

きる kiru

たべる taberu

はなす hanasu

ほる horu

はこぶ hakob

のむ nomu

つくる tsukuru

とぶ tobu

はう hau

おどる odoru

あらう arau

あむ am

あそぶ asobu

みる miru

のぼる noboru

とる toru

はねる haneru

ねる neru

ぬう nuu

まつ matsu

んかする kenka-suru

かくれる kakureru

ぬう yomu

かう kau

うりする ōri-suru

うたう utau

ふく fuku

ひく hiku

おす osu

はく haku

つむ tsumu

ろぶ korobu

あるく aruku

はしる hashiru

すわる suwaru

43

はんたいのことば
hantai no kotoba

よい yoi

わるい warui

いちばんうえ ichiban-ue

いちばんした ichiban-shita

ふとった futotta

やせた yaseta

すくない sukunai

おおい ōi

つめたい tsumetai

あつい atsui

きたない kitanai

きれい kirei

あく aku

しまる shimaru

さいしょ saisho

さいご saigo

とおい tōi

ちかい chi

ぬれている nureteiru

かわいてい kawaiteiru

うえ ue

した shita

ちいさい chiisai

おおきい

ひだり hidari

44

と soto

なか naka

やさしい yasashii

むずかしい muzukashii

から kara

いっぱい ippai

やわらかい yawarakai

かたい katai

まえ mae

たかい takai

おそい osoi

はやい hayai

うしろ ushiro

ひくい hikui

ながい nagai

みじかい mijikai

かれている kareteiru

いきている ikiteiru

くらい kurai

あかるい akarui

にかい nikai

ふるい furui

みぎ migi

あたらしい atarashii

いっかい ikkai

45

いろいろなひ iroirona-hi

げつようび
getsu-yōbi

かようび
ka-yōbi

すいようび
sui-yōbi

もくようび
moku-yōbi

きんようび
kin-yōbi

どようび
do-yōbi

にちようび
nichi-yōbi

カレンダー
karendā

あさ asa

たいよう
taiyō

ゆうがた yūgata

よる yoru

うちゅう uchū

わくせい
wakusei

うちゅうせん
uchū-sen

つき tsuki

ほし hoshi

てんたいぼうえんきょう
tentai-bōenkyō

とくべつなひ tokubetsuna-hi

たんじょうび
tanjōbi

プレゼント
purezento

ろうそく rōsoku

バースデーカード
bāsudē-kādo

バースデークーキ
bāsudē-keki

きゅうか kyūka

けっこんしき kekkon-shiki

ブライズ・メイド
buraizu meido

はなよめ
hana-yome

はなむこ
hana-muko

カメラ kamera

カメラマン
kamera-man

クリスマス kurisumasu

トナカイ
tonakai

そり sori

サンタクロース santa-kurōsu

クリスマスツリー
kurisumasu-tsurii

てんき _{tenki}

たいよう taiyō

くも kur

そら sorc

かさ kasa

あめ ame

かみなり kaminari

きり kiri

ゆき yuki

つゆ tsuyu

かぜ kaze

かすみ kasumi

しも shimo

にじ niji

きせつ _{kisetsu}

はる haru

なつ natsu

あき aki

ふゆ fuyu

ペット petto

ハムスター hamusutā

じゅうい jūi

いぬごや inu-gora

モルモット morumotto

こいぬ ko-inu

いぬ inu

セキセイインコ sekisei-inko

えさ esa

おうむ ōmu

くちばし kuchibashi

カナリア kanaria

うさぎ usagi

とりかご torikago

ねこ neko

バスケット basuketto

ねずみ nezumi

こねこ ko-neko

ぎゅうにゅう gyūnyū

きんぎょ kingyo

49

スポーツとうんどう supōtsu to undō

ボートこぎ
bōto-kogi

スノウボード sunō-bōdo

セーリング sēringu

ウィンドサーフィン
uindo-sāfin

バスケットボール
basuketto-bōru

ラケット
raketto

クリケット
kuriketto

からて karate

バット ba

たいそう taisō

ボール
bōru

テニス tenisu

アメリカンフットボール
amerikan-futtobōru

つりざお tsuri-zao

ダンス dansu

やきゅう yak

つり tsuri

えさ esa

ラグビー ragubii

とびこみ tobikomi

プール pūru

レース

すいえい suiei

まと mato

ハングライダー hanguraidā

アーチェリー ācherii

ヘルメット herumetto

ジョギング jogingu

サイクリング saikuringu

ロッククライミング rokku-karaimingu

ロッカー rokkā

じゅうどう jūdō

うま uma

こうま ko-uma

こういしつ kōi-shitsu

サッカー sakkā

じょうば jōba

バドミントン badominton

スケートぐつ sukēto-gutsu

たっきゅう takkyū

アイススケート aisu-sukēto

ストック sutokku

スキーリフト sukii-rifuto

スキーいた sukii-ita

スキー sukii

すもう sumō

51

いろ iro

オレンジいろ orenji-iro

みどり midori

くろ kuro

はいいろ hai-iro

あか aka

ちゃいろ cha-iro

しろ shiro

あお ao

ピンク pinku

むらさき murasaki

きいろ k

かたち katachi

ちょうほうけい chōhōkei

まる maru

ひしがた hishigata

えんすい ensui

ほしがた hoshi-gata

りっぽうたい rippōta

だえんけい daenkei

さんかくけい sankakukei

せいほうけい seihōkei

みかづきがた mikazuki-gata

かず kazu

いち ichi

に ni

さん san

し shi

ご go

ろく roku

しち shichi

はち hachi

きゅう kyū

0 じゅう jū

1 じゅういち jūichi

2 じゅうに jūni

3 じゅうさん jūsan

4 じゅうし jūshi

5 じゅうご jūgo

6 じゅうろく jūroku

7 じゅうしち jūshichi

8 じゅうはち jūhachi

9 じゅうきゅう jūkyū

0 にじゅう nijū

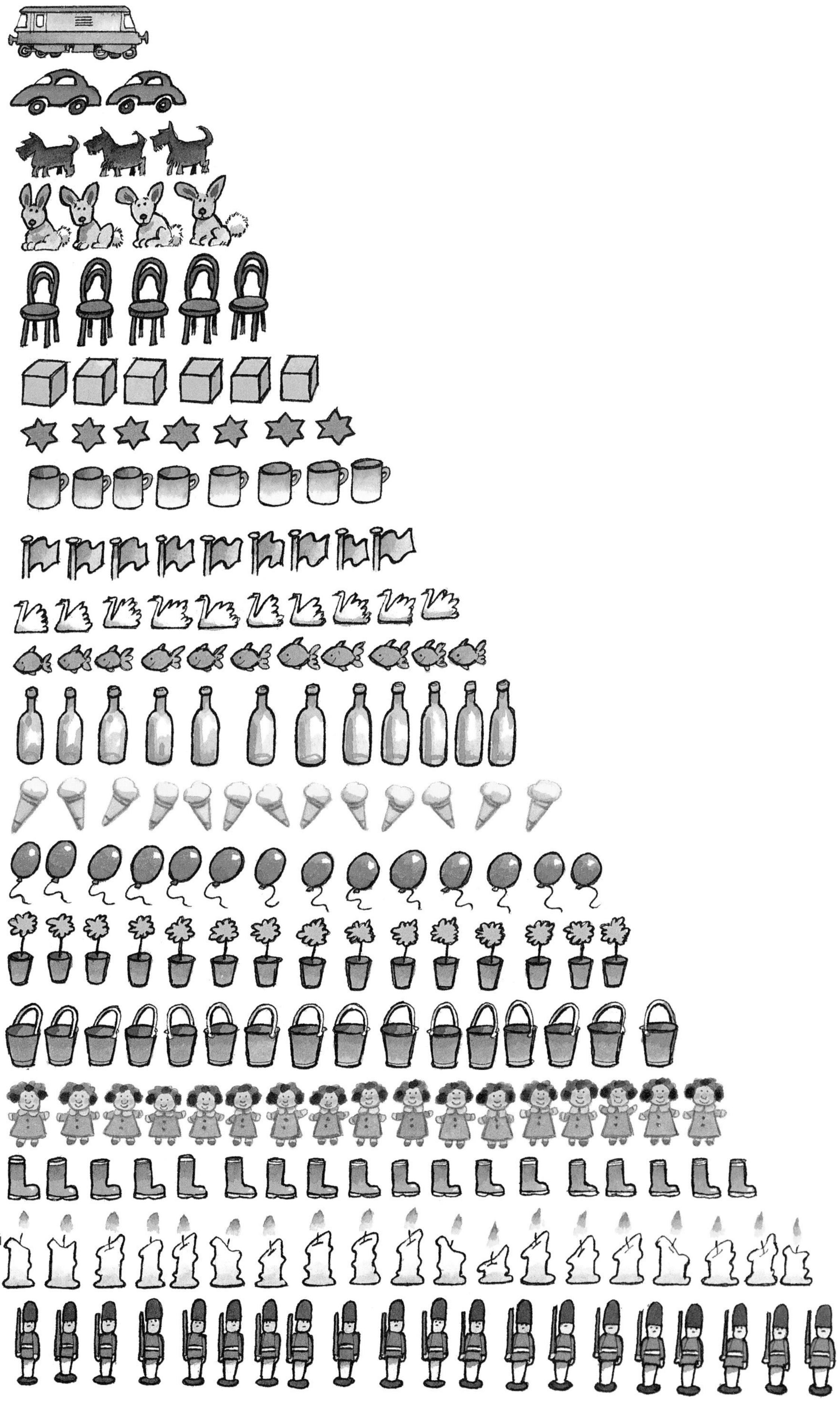

ゆうえんち yūenchi

メリーゴーランド
merii-gō-rando

マット
matto

すべりだい suberidai

かんらんしゃ karansha

おばけやしき obake-yashiki

ポップコーン
poppu-kōn

わなげ wanage

ジェットコースター jetto-kōsutā

しゃげき shageki

ゴーカート
gō-kāto

わたあめ wata-ame

サーカス sākasu

つなわたり tsunawatari

ぼう bō

くうちゅうブランコ kūchū-buranko

ワイヤーロープ waiyā-rōpu

なわばしご nawabashigo

あんぜんネット anzen-netto

ちりんしゃのり ichirinsha-nori

うさぎ usagi

アクロバット akurabatto

ちょうきょうし chōkyōshi

いぬ inu

わ wa

シルクハット shiruku-hatto

きょくげいし kyokugeisha

ちょうねくたい chō-nekutai

バンド bando

うまのり umanori

ピエロ piero

55

About *kanji*

The Japanese signs used in this book (see page two) are called *kana*, and they are based on sounds. They are simple signs that you use when you first learn Japanese. Normally, they are used mixed in with some other, more complicated signs, called kanji or "characters". Each *kanji* represents a word or an idea.

When people first started to write, they used simple pictures of things to show what they were writing about. This is how *kanji* started, and some *kanji* signs still look like what they represent. For example: 木 this *kanji* means "tree". It can also be written using *kana*, き , and said as "ki". 森 this *kanji* means "forest". Notice that it is made from three "tree" *kanji*.

There are many *kanji*. To read a newspaper, you have to know around 2000. It takes a few years to learn them, so it is best to start with *kana*, learning a few of these at a time.

About the word list

In this list, you can find all the Japanese words in the book. For each double page, the Japanese words are shown written in our alphabet. Next to each word you can see its translation (what it means in English).

The translations match the pictures, so if the picture shows leaves, the translation is "leaves", not "leaf". In Japanese, though, there is usually no difference between singular and plural (one and many), so "leaf" and "leaves" are both "ha".

To know how you should say the Japanese words, look at page two or go to the Usborne Quicklinks Website at **www.usborne-quicklinks.com** and type in the keywords "1000 japanese". There you can listen to all the words in this book, spoken by a native Japanese person.

Internet note for parents and guardians

Please ensure that your children read and follow the Internet safety guidelines displayed on the Usborne Quicklinks Website.

The links in Usborne Quicklinks are regularly reviewed and updated. However, the content of a website may change at any time and Usborne Publishing is not responsible for the content on any website other than its own. We recommend that children are supervised while on the Internet, that they do not use Internet Chat Rooms, and that you use Internet filtering software to block unsuitable material. For more information, see the **Net Help** area on the Usborne Quicklinks Website.

pages 4-5

uchi	**home**
yokushitsu	**bathroom**
ofuro	bathtub
sekken	soap
jaguchi	faucet
toiretto-pepā	toilet pape
ha-burashi	toothbrush
mizu	water
toire	toilet
suponji	sponge
senmendai	sink
shawā	shower
taoru	towel
neri-hamigaki	toothpaste
rajio	radio
ima	**living room**
kusshon	cushion
shiidii	CD
jūtan	carpet
sofā	sofa
hiitā	radiator
bideo	video
genkan	**hall**
shinbun	newspaper
tēburu	table
tegami	letters
kaidan	stairs
denwa	telephone
kōto-kake	hat pegs
shinshitsu	**bedroom**
e	pictures
denki-sutando	lamp
burashi	brush
kagami	mirror
hikidashi	chest of dr
makura	pillow
yōfuku-dansu	wardrobe
shikimono	rug
shiitsu	sheet
kushi	comb
kakebuton	comforter
isu	chair
beddo	bed

koro	kitchen
ɔ	refrigerator
	cups
	clock
ake	stool
	teaspoons
i	light switch
	laundry detergent
	key
	door
	vacuum cleaner
	saucepans
	forks
n	apron
dai	ironing board
	trash
	dish towel
appu	coffee cups
hi	matches
i	scrub brush
	bowls
-ire	cupboard
	iron
	plates
	spoons
	cooker
an	frying pan
ra	saucers
shi	drawer
ri	dustpan
kuki	washing machine
	broom
	tiles
	dust cloth
	mop
u	knives
	kettle
shi	sink

	yard
guruma	wheelbarrow
ko	beehive
umuri	snail

renga	bricks
hato	pigeon
sukkopu	spade
tentō-mushi	ladybug
gomi-ire	trash can
tane	seeds
koya	shed
mimizu	worm
hana	flowers
supurinkurā	sprinkler
kana-guwa	hoe
suzume-bachi	wasp
kusa	grass
ubaguruma	baby buggy
hashigo	ladder
takibi	bonfire
hōsu	hose
onshitsu	greenhouse
ko-eda	sticks
tori no su	bird's nest
kumade	rake
kemushi	caterpillar
kemuri	smoke
ki	tree
ha	leaves
ko-michi	path
shibakariki	lawn mower
mataguwa	fork
ike-gaki	hedge
hone	bone
shaberu	trowel
mitsubachi	honeybee
jōro	watering can

pages 10-11

sagyōba	workshop
manriki	vise
kami-yasuri	sandpaper
doriru	drill
hashigo	ladder
nokogiri	saw
ogakuzu	sawdust
karendā	calendar
dōgu-bako	toolbox
nejimawashi	screwdriver

ita	plank
kanna-kuzu	wood shavings
oritatami-naifu	pocketknife
zaimoku	wood
kugi	nails
sagyōdai	workbench
bin	jars
kan-na	wood plane
penki-kan	paint can
yasuri	file
hanmā	hammer
makijaku	tape measure
ono	axe
hae	fly
taru	barrel
kumo no su	cobweb
natto	nuts
boruto	bolts
kumo	spider
byō	tacks
neji	screws

pages 12-13

tōri	street
mise	store
ana	hole
kissaten	café
kyūkyū sha	ambulance
hodō	sidewalk
antena	(TV) antenna
entotsu	chimney
yane	roof
shaberu-ka	digger
hoteru	hotel
otoko-no-hito	man
patokā	police car
dokan	pipes
doriru	drill
gakkō	school
undō-jō	playground
jitensha	bicycle
shōbō-sha	fire engine
keikan	policeman
kuruma	car
onna-no-ko	woman

57

gaitō	lamp post	ayatsuri-ningyō	puppets	ubaguruma	stroller
apāto	apartments	bii-dama	marbles	tsuchi	dirt
ōtobai	motorcycle	chokin-bako	money box	sukētobōdo	skateboard
fumidan	steps	mokuba	rocking horse	akachan	baby
ichiba	market	rēshingu-kā	racing car	benchi	bench
ie	house	omen	masks		
torērā	trailer	rōrā	steamroller		
rōrā	steamroller	kaoyō-enogu	face paints		
raito-ban	van	yotto	boat		
eiga-kan	movie theater	parashūto	parachute		
kōtsū-shingō	traffic lights	yumi	bow		
torakku	truck	hāmonika	harmonica		
kōjō	factory				
ōdan-hodō	crosswalk				
takushii	taxi				
basu	bus				

pages 18-19

dōbutsuen — **zoo**

panda	panda
washi	eagle
tsubasa	wing
kaba	hippopota(mus)
kōmori	bat
gorira	gorilla
kangarū	kangaroo
mae-ashi	(front) paw
saru	monkey
shippo	tail
ōkami	wolf
wani	crocodile
pengin	penguin
hyōzan	iceberg
kuma	bear
perikan	pelican
dachō	ostrich
hane	feathers
iruka	dolphin
kirin	giraffe
raion	lion
raion-no-ko	lion cubs
shika	deer
tsuno	antlers
rakuda	camel
azarashi	seal
shiro-kuma	polar bear
kame	tortoise
zō	elephant
zō no hana	trunk
sai	rhinoceros
baffarō	buffalo
yagi	goat
shima-uma	zebra
same	shark
biibā	beaver
hebi	snake

pages 14-15

omochaya — **toy shop**

kisha-setto	train set
saikoro	dice
tate-bue	recorder
robotto	robot
doramu	drums
nekkuresu	necklace
kamera	camera
biizu	beads
ningyō	dolls
gitā	guitar
yubiwa	ring
ningyō no ie	doll's house
fue	whistle
tsumiki	blocks
o-shiro	castle
sensuikan	submarine
toranpetto	trumpet
yane	arrows
kurēn	crane
nendo	clay
teppō	gun
heitai	soldiers
enogu	paints
roketto	rocket
uchū-hikōshi	spacemen
piano	piano

pages 16-17

kōen — **park**

buranko	swings
sunaba	sandbox
pikunikku	picnic
tako	kite
aisukuriimu	ice cream
inu	dog
mon	gate
ko-michi	path
kaeru	frog
suberidai	slide
otamajakushi	tadpoles
ike	lake
rōrā-sukēto	roller skates
shigemi	bush
kadan	flower bed
hakuchō	swans
hikizuna	dog leash
kamo	ducks
ki	trees
nawatobi	jump rope
ko-gamo	ducklings
mizu-tamari	puddle
ito	string
yotto	yacht
bōru	ball
saku	fence
tori	birds
sanrinsha	tricycle
kodomo	children
shiisō	seesaw

me	shark		
jira	whale		
ra	tiger		
ō	leopard		

pages 20-21

okō	travel		
i	station		
nro	train track		
kan-sha	engine		
ruma-dome	buffers		
aryō	railway cars		
tenshu	train engineer		
sha	freight train		
uratto-hōmu	platform		
ashō	ticket inspector		
tsukēsu	suitcase		
opu-hanbaiki	ticket machine		
ingō	signals		
ukkusakku	backpack		
asorin-sutando	gas station		
eddo-raito	headlights		
njin	engine		
arin	wheel		
atterii	battery		
asorin-sha	oil tanker		
pana	wrench		
iya	tire		
on-neto	hood (car)		
ru	oil		
asorin-ire	gas pump		
kkā-sha	tow truck		
asorin	gasoline		
ranku	trunck (car)		
ensha	car wash		
kōjō	airport		
airotto	pilot		
uchuwādo	flight attendant (male)		
anseitō	control tower		
assōro	runway		
uchuwādesu	flight attendant (female)		
kōki	plane		
erikoputā	helicopter		

pages 22-23

inaka	country		
fūsha-goya	windmill		
netsu-kikyū	hot-air balloon		
chō-cho	butterfly		
tokage	lizard		
ishi	stones		
kitsune	fox		
ogawa	stream		
michi-shirube	signpost		
hari-nezumi	hedgehog		
sui-mon	lock (canal)		
risu	squirrel		
mori	forest		
anaguma	badger		
kawa	river		
michi	road		
iwa	rocks		
hikigaeru	toad		
densha	train		
kyanpingu-kā	camper		
oka	hill		
tsuri-bito	fisherman		
mogura	mole		
kogitsune	fox cubs		
ton-neru	tunnel		
fukurō	owl		
taki	waterfall		
fune	barge		
hashi	bridge		
ga	moth		
mura	village		
maruta	logs		
unga	canal		
tento	tents		
yama	mountain		

pages 24-25

nōjō	farm		
hoshikusa no yama	haystack		
bokuyō-ken	sheepdog		
ahiru	ducks		
ko-hitsuji	lambs		
ike	pond		
hiyoko	chicks		

yane-ura	loft		
buta-goya	pigsty		
o-ushi	bull		
ahiru no ko	ducklings		
niwatori-goya	hen house		
torakutā	tractor		
gachō	geese		
tanku-rōrii	tanker		
naya	barn		
nukarumi	mud		
te-oshi-guruma	cart		
hoshi-kusa	hay		
hitsuji	sheep		
wara-taba	straw bales		
uma	horse		
buta	pigs		
nōka	farmhouse		
kakashi	scarecrow		
shichimenchō	turkeys		
hitsujikai	shepherdess		
ko-buta	piglets		
uma-goya	stable		
kaju-en	orchard		
suki	plough		
me-ushi	cow		
ushi-goya	cowshed		
sadoru	saddle		
hei	fence		
ko-ushi	calf		
mendori	hens		
sōgen	field		
nōfu	farmer		
ondori	rooster		

pages 26-27

umibe	seaside		
yotto	sailboat		
umi	sea		
ōru	oar		
tōdai	lighthouse		
shaberu	spade		
baketsu	bucket		
hitode	starfish		
suna no shiro	sandcastle		
biichi-parasoru	beach umbrella		

hata	flag	e	drawing	ringo	apple
sen-in	sailor	doa no totte	door handle	terebi	television
kani	crab	shokubutsu	plant	nemaki	nightgown
kamome	seagull	chikyūgi	globe	pajama	pajamas
shima	island	onna no ko	girl	orenji	orange (fruit)
mōtā-bōto	motorboat	kureyon	crayons	**isha**	**doctor**
suijō-sukii	water skiing	denki-sutando	lamp	tisshu-pēpā	tissues
mizugi	swimsuit	iizeru	easel	manga	comic
oiru-tankā	oil tanker	buraindo	blind	machiai-shitsu	waiting room
hamabe	beach	kami	paper	tsue	cane
bōto	rowboat	suisō	aquarium	omutsu	diaper
dekki-cheā	deck chair	bajji	badge	kādo	cards
sakana	fish	arufabetto	alphabet	nashi	pear
roba	donkey	nōto	notebook	omocha	toys
mizu-kaki	flippers	yuka	floor	kago	basket
tsuri-bune	fishing boat	kabe	wall	budō	grapes
kai	paddle	tenjō	ceiling	banana	banana
ami	net	fude	brush	bando-eido	bandaid
kaisō	seaweed	chizu	map	konpyūtā	computer
koishi	pebbles	hako	box	shitsunai-baki	slippers
rōpu	rope	sensei	teacher		
kanū	canoe	gomibako	wastepaper basket		
fune	ship	howaito-bōdo	board	**pages 32-33**	
gake	cliff			**pātii**	**party**
bōshi	sun hat			fūsen	balloon
nami	waves	**pages 30-31**		chokorēto	chocolate
kai	shell	**byōin**	**hospital**	okashi	candy
		kangofu	nurse	mado	window
pages 28-29		dasshimen	cotton	hanabi	fireworks
gakkō	**school**	kusuri	medicine	ribon	ribbon
hasami	scissors	erebētā	elevator	kēki	cake
keisan	calculation	gaun	bathrobe	sutorō	straw
keshigomu	eraser	matsuba-zue	crutches	rōsoko	candle
monosashi	ruler	jōzai	pills	kami-gusari	paper chain
shashin	photographs	o-bon	tray	omocha	toys
feruto-pen	felt-tip pens	ude-dokei	watch	sandoicchi	sandwich
gabyō	thumb tacks	taionkei	thermometer	batā	butter
enogu	paints	kāten	curtain	bisuketto	cookie
otoko no ko	boy	gibusu	cast	chiizu	cheese
enpitsu	pencil	hōtai	bandage	pan	bread
tsukue	desk	kuruma-isu	wheelchair	tēburu-kurosu	tablecloth
hon	books	jiguzō-pazuru	jigsaw	denkyū	light bulb
pen	pen	isha	doctor	ichigo	strawberry
nori	glue	chūshaki	syringe	ki-ichigo	raspberry
chōku	chalk	tedibea	teddy bear	furūtsu-jūsu	fruit juice

kuranbo	cherry	puramu	plum	**pages 38-39**	
gurumi	costume	tamago	eggs	**watashi**	**me, I**
teto-chippusu	potato chips	kaimono-bukuro	carrier bag	atama	head
sēji	sausage	chiizu	cheese	kami	hair
ssetto-tēpu	cassette tape	kudamo	fruit	kao	face
rami	salami	yasai	vegetables	mayuge	eyebrow
kan	tangerine			me	eye
rezento	presents			hana	nose
		pages 36-37		hoho	cheek
		tabemono	**food**	kuchi	mouth
ges 34-35		asa-gohan	breakfast	kuchibiru	lips
nise	**grocery store**	hiru-gohan	lunch	ha	teeth
rēpu-furūtsu	grapefruit	kōhii	coffee	shita	tongue
jin	carrot	yude-tamago	boiled egg	ago	chin
rifurawā	cauliflower	medama-yaki	fried egg	ude	arm
gi	Chinese chive	tōsuto	toast	hiji	elbow
asshurūmu	mushroom	jamu	jam	onaka	tummy
ūri	cucumber	kōn-furēku	cornflakes	mimi	ears
mon	lemon	kokoa	hot chocolate	kubi	neck
rori	celery	kuriimu	cream	kata	shoulders
urikotto	apricot	gyūnyū	milk	ashi	leg
eron	melon	satō	sugar	tsumasaki	toes
manegi	onion	kōcha	tea	ashi	foot
abetsu	cabbage	hachimitsu	honey	hiza	knee
omo	peach	shio	salt	mune	chest
tasu	lettuce	koshō	pepper	senaka	back
ya-endō	peas	hotto-kēki	pancakes	oshiri	bottom
mato	tomato	rōru-pan	bread rolls	te	hand
ga-imo	potatoes	ban-gohan	supper	oya-yubi	thumb
rensō	spinach	hamu	ham	yubi	fingers
gen	beans	sūpu	soup	**watashi no yōfuku**	**my clothes**
i	checkout	omuretsu	omelette	sokkusu	socks
bocha	pumpkin	hashi	chopsticks	pantsu	underwear
to	shopping cart	sarada	salad	ranning-shatsu	undershirt
nzume	cans	hanbāgā	hamburger	zubon	pants
kane	money	tori-niku	chicken	jiipan	jeans
ifu	coin purse	gohan	rice	tiishatsu	T-shirt
ndo-baggu	purse	sōsu	sauce	sukāto	skirt
toru	bottles	supagettii	spaghetti	shatsu	shirt
suketto	basket	masshu-poteto	mashed potato	nekutai	tie
guruto	yogurt	piza	pizza	hanzubon	shorts
inappuru	pineapple	furaido-poteto	french fries	taitsu	tights
ku	meat	dezāto	pudding	doresu	dress
n	jars			sētā	sweater
kari	scales			torēnā	sweatshirt
mugiko	flour			kādigan	cardigan

mafurā	scarf	**kazoku**	**family**	kenka-suru	fight
hankachi	handkerchief	musuko	son	neru	sleep
suniikā	sneakers	otōto	younger brother	toru	take
kutsu	shoes	ani	older brother	nuu	sew
sandaru	sandals	musume	daughter	haneru	skip
būtsu	boots	ane	older sister	matsu	wait
tebukuro	gloves	imoto	younger sister	ryōri-suru	cook
poketto	pockets	haha	mother	kakureru	hide
beruto	belt	tsuma	wife	utau	sing
bakkuru	buckle	chichi	father	yomu	read
jippā	zipper	otto	husband	kau	buy
kutsuhimo	shoelace	oba	aunt	osu	push
botan	buttons	oji	uncle	hiku	pull
botan no ana	button holes	itoko	cousin	haku	sweep
kōto	coat	sofu	grandfather	tsumu	pick
jaketto	jacket	sobo	grandmother	fuku	blow
yakyū-bō	baseball cap			korobu	fall
bōshi	hat			aruku	walk

pages 42-43

dōsa	**doing things**	hashiru	run
hohoemu	smile	suwaru	sit

pages 40-41

hito — **people**

danyū	actor
joyū	actress
kokku	chef
kashu	singers
dansā	dancers
nikuya	butcher
keikan	policeman
fujin-keikan	policewoman
uchū-hikōshi	astronaut
daiku	carpenter
shōbōshi	firefighter
gaka	artist
saibankan	judge
seibishi	mechanics
biyōshi	hairdresser
torakku no untenshu	truck driver
basu no untenshu	bus driver
ueitā	waiter
ueitoresu	waitress
yūbin-ya	mail carrier
penkiya	painter
haisha	dentist
sensuifu	frogman
panya	baker

dōsa doing things
hohoemu	smile
naku	cry
kangaeru	think
kiku	listen
warau	laugh
uketoru	catch
nageru	throw
kowasu	break
kaku	paint
kaku	write
tataki-kiru	chop
kiru	cut
taberu	eat
hanasu	talk
horu	dig
hakobu	carry
nomu	drink
tsukuru	make
tobu	jump
hau	crawl
odoru	dance
arau	wash
amu	knit
asobu	play
miru	watch
noboru	climb

pages 44-45

hantai no kotoba — **opposite**

yoi	good
warui	bad
tsumetai	cold
atsui	hot
tōi	far
chikai	near
nureteiru	wet
kawaiteiru	dry
ichiban-ue	top
ichiban-shita	bottom
kitanai	dirty
kirei	clean
ue	over
shita	under
futotta	fat
yaseta	thin
aku	open
shimaru	closed
chiisai	small
ōkii	big
sukunai	few
ōi	many

₁o	first	
₁o	last	
₁ri	left	
	right	
₁	out	
₁	in	
₁shii	easy	
₁ukashii	difficult	
₁	empty	
₁i	full	
₁arakai	soft	
₁i	hard	
₁	front	
₁o	back	
₁i	high	
	low	
₁	slow	
₁ai	fast	
₁ai	long	
₁ai	short	
₁teiru	dead	
₁ru	alive	
₁i	dark	
₁rui	light	
₁ashii	new	
	old	
₁	up	
₁	down	

es 46-47

₁ana-hi	**days**
₁u-yōbi	Monday
₁ōbi	Tuesday
₁ōbi	Wednesday
₁u-yōbi	Thursday
₁ōbi	Friday
₁ōbi	Saturday
₁i-yōbi	Sunday
₁ndā	calendar
	morning
₁ō	sun
₁ata	evening
₁	night
₁ū	space
₁usei	planet

uchū-sen	spaceship
tentai-bōenkyō	telescope
tsuki	moon
hoshi	star
tokubetsuna-hi	**special days**
tanjōbi	birthday
purezento	present
rōsoku	candle
bāsudē-keki	birthday cake
bāsudē-kādo	birthday card
kyūka	vacation
kekkon-shiki	wedding day
buraizu meido	bridesmaid
hana-yome	bride
hana-muko	bridegroom
kamera-man	photographer
kamera	camera
kurisumasu	Christmas day
santa-kurōsu	Santa Claus
sori	sleigh
tonakai	reindeer
kurisumasu-tsurii	Christmas tree

pages 48-49

tenki	**weather**
ame	rain
kasa	umbrella
kaminari	lightning
kiri	fog
taiyō	sun
sora	sky
kumo	clouds
yuki	snow
tsuyu	dew
kaze	wind
kasumi	mist
shimo	frost
niji	rainbow
kisetsu	**seasons**
haru	spring
natsu	summer
aki	autumn
fuyu	winter
petto	**pets**
hamusutā	hamster

morumotto	guinea pig
jūi	vet
inu	dog
inu-goya	kennel
ko-inu	puppy
esa	food
sekisei-inko	budgerigar
ōmu	parrot
kuchibashi	beak
usagi	rabbit
kanaria	canary
torikago	birdcage
nezumi	mouse
ko-neko	kitten
neko	cat
basuketto	basket
gyūnyū	milk
kingyo	goldfish

pages 50-51

supōtsu to undō	**sports & exercise**
basuketto-bōru	basketball
bōto-kogi	rowing
sēringu	sailing
uindo-sāfin	windsurfing
sunō-bōdo	snowboarding
tenisu	tennis
raketto	racket
american-futtobōru	American football
taisō	exercises
kuriketto	cricket (sport)
karate	karate
tsuri	fishing
tsuri-zao	fishing rod
esa	bait
ragubii	rugby
dansu	dance
yakyū	baseball
batto	bat
bōru	ball
suiei	swimming
tobikomi	diving, jumping
pūru	swimming pool
rēsu	race
ācherii	archery

mato	target	maru	circle	bō	pole
hanguraidā	hang-gliding	rippōtai	cube	nawabashigo	rope ladd
jūdō	judo	mikazuki-gata	crescent	anzen-netto	safety net
jogingu	jogging	**kazu**	**numbers**	kyokugeishi	juggler
saikuringu	cycling	ichi	one	chōkyōshi	ring maste
rokku-kuraimingu	climbing	ni	two	wa	hoop
herumetto	helmet	san	three	inu	dog
badominton	badminton	shi	four	usagi	rabbit
sakkā	soccer	go	five	shiruku-hatto	top hat
jōba	riding	roku	six	bando	band
uma	horse	shichi	seven	umanori	bareback
ko-uma	pony	hachi	eight	piero	clown
kōi-shitsu	changing room	kyū	nine	chō-nekutai	bow tie
rokkā	locker	jū	ten		
takkyū	table tennis	jūichi	eleven		
aisu-sukēto	ice skating	jūni	twelve		
sukēto-gutsu	ice skates	jūsan	thirteen		
sukii	skiing	jūshi	fourteen		
sukii-ita	ski	jūgo	fifteen		
sutokko	ski pole	jūroku	sixteen		
sukii-rifuto	chairlift	jūshichi	seventeen		
sumō	sumo wrestling	jūhachi	eighteen		
		jūkyū	nineteen		
		nijū	twenty		

pages 52-53

iro	**colors**			
cha-iro	brown			
shiro	white			
kuro	black			
ao	blue			
pinku	pink			
orenji-iro	orange			
hai-iro	gray			
murasaki	purple			
midori	green			
aka	red			
ki-iro	yellow			
katachi	**shapes**			
hishigata	diamond			
daenkei	oval			
ensui	cone			
sankakukei	triangle			
chōhōkei	rectangle			
hoshi-gata	star			
seihōkei	square			

pages 54-55

yūenchi	**fairground**
kanransha	Ferris wheel
merii-gō-rando	merry-go-round
suberidai	slide
matto	mat
wanage	ring toss
obake-yashiki	haunted house ride
poppu-kōn	popcorn
jetto-kōsutā	roller coaster
shageki	rifle range
gō-kāto	dodgems
wata-ame	cotton candy
sākasu	**circus**
ichirinsha-nori	unicyclist
akurobatto	acrobats
kūchū-buranko	trapeze
tsunawatari	tightrope walker
waiyā-rōpu	tightrope

This revised edition first published in 1995 b
Usborne Publishing Ltd, Usborne House,
83-85 Saffron Hill, London EC1N 8RT, Engla
www.usborne.com
Based on a previous title first published in 1
Copyright © 2002, 1995, 1979 Usborne Pub
First published in America in March 1996.
This American edition published in 2003.

Printed in Italy.